NINJA HATTORI

COLOURING BOOK

YOUTHBOOKS

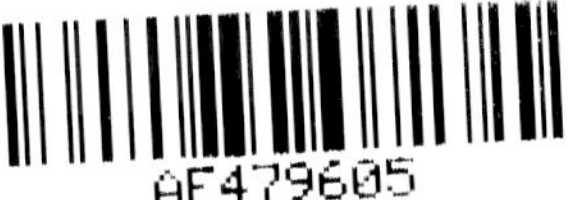

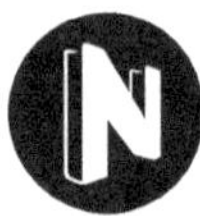

Copyright © Youthbooks
All Rights Reserved.

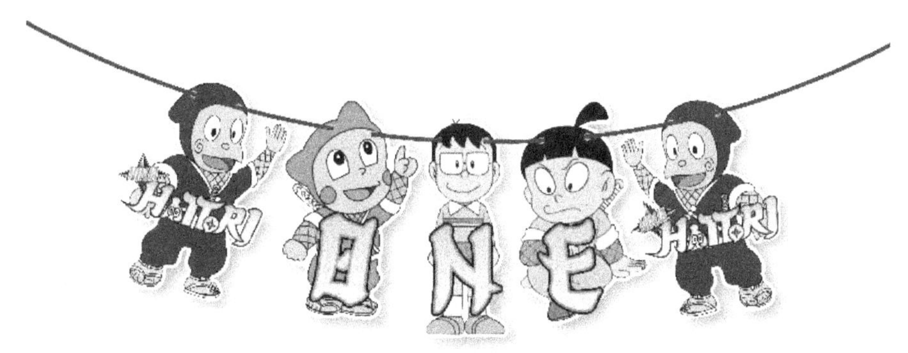
HATTORI
ONE
HATTORI

Contents

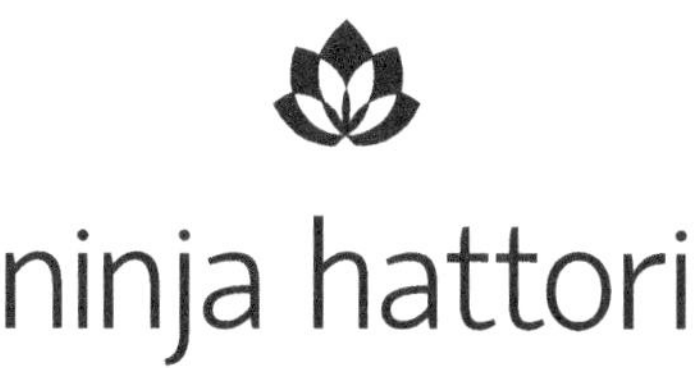

ninja hattori

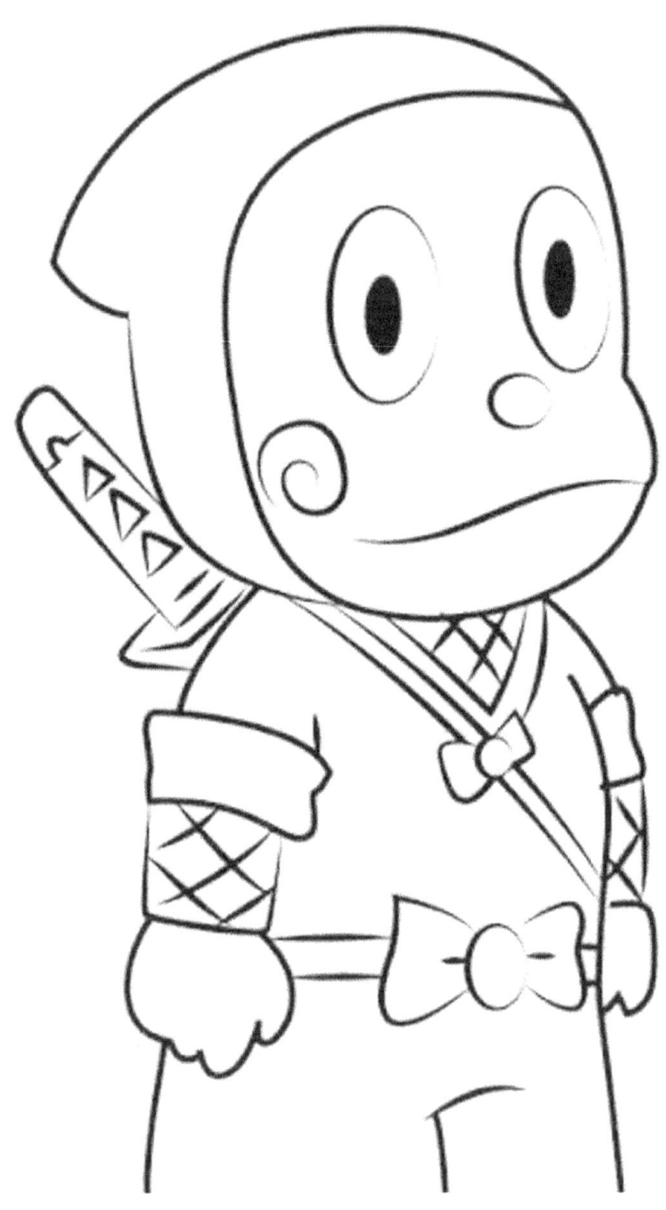

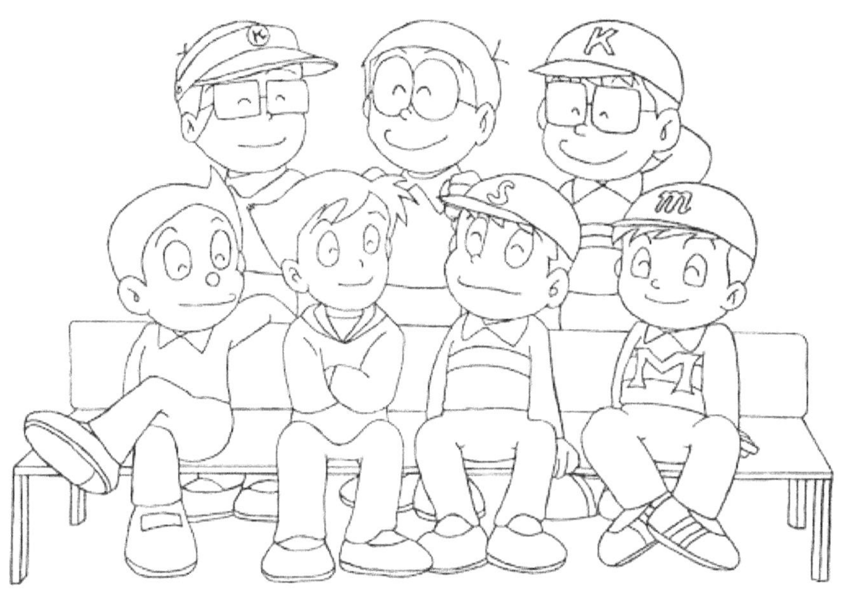

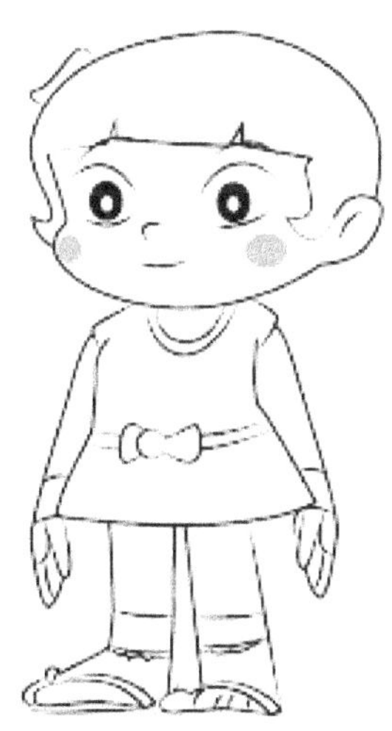

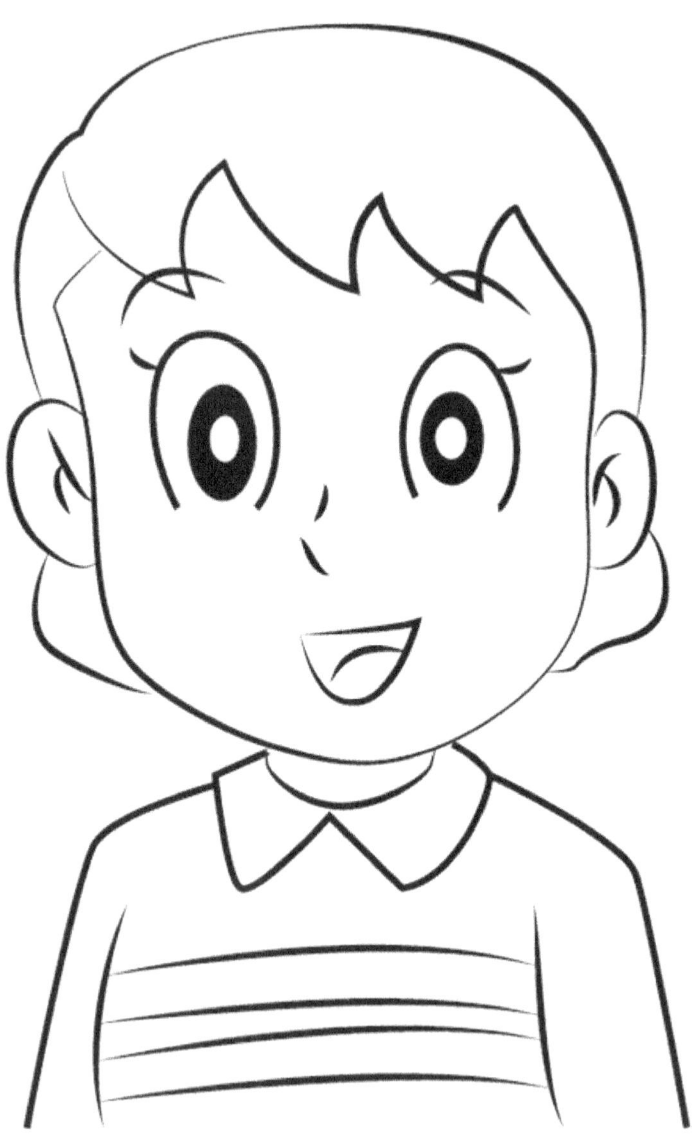

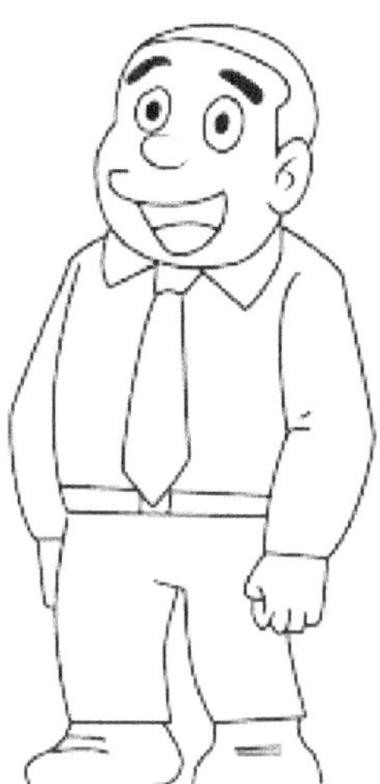

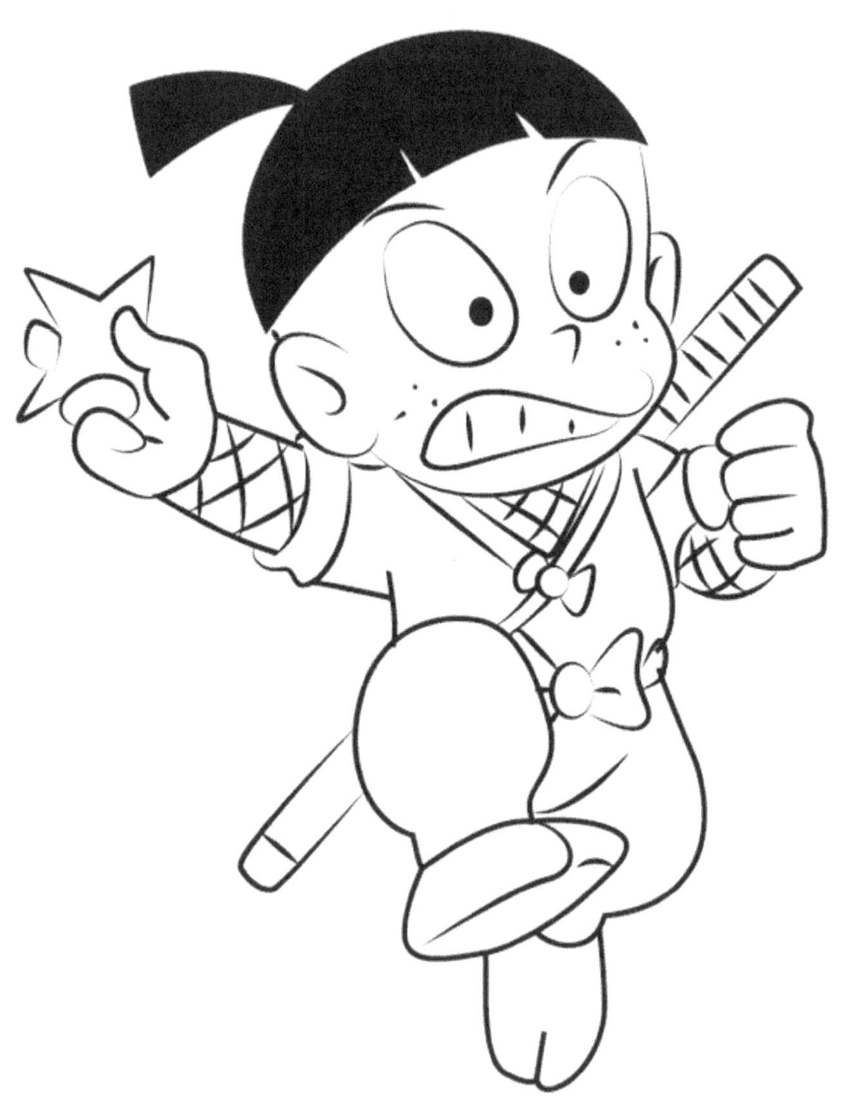

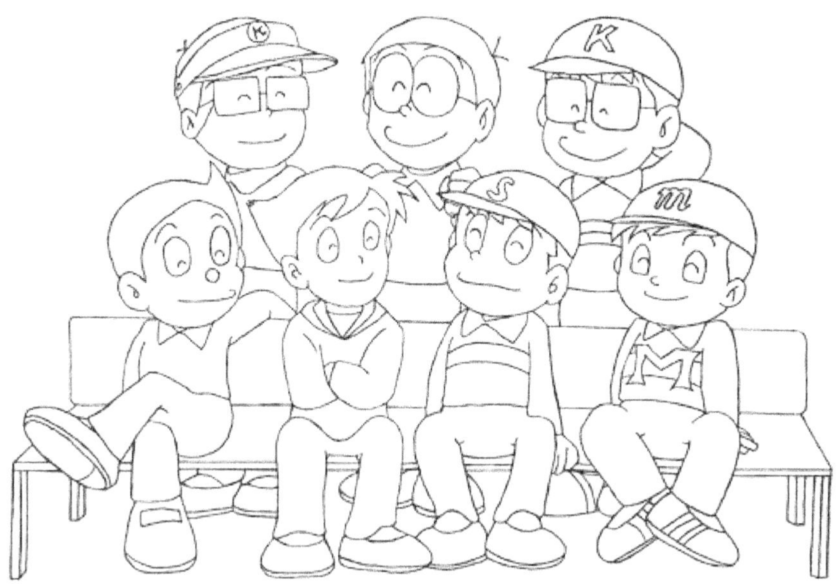

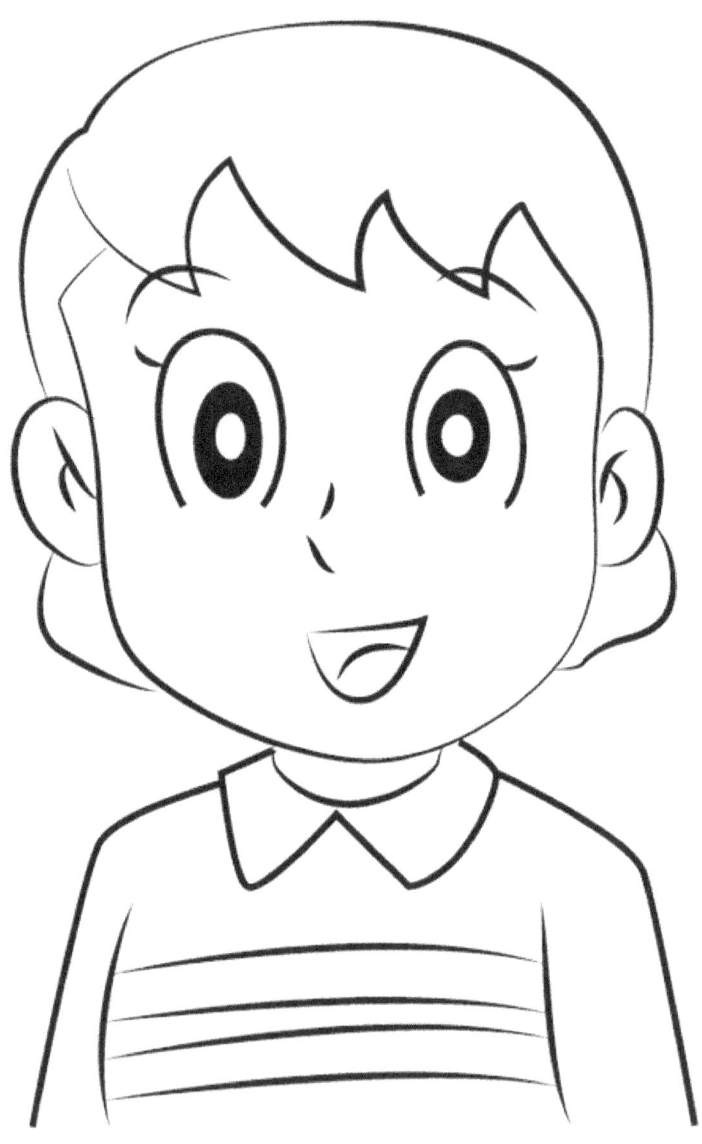

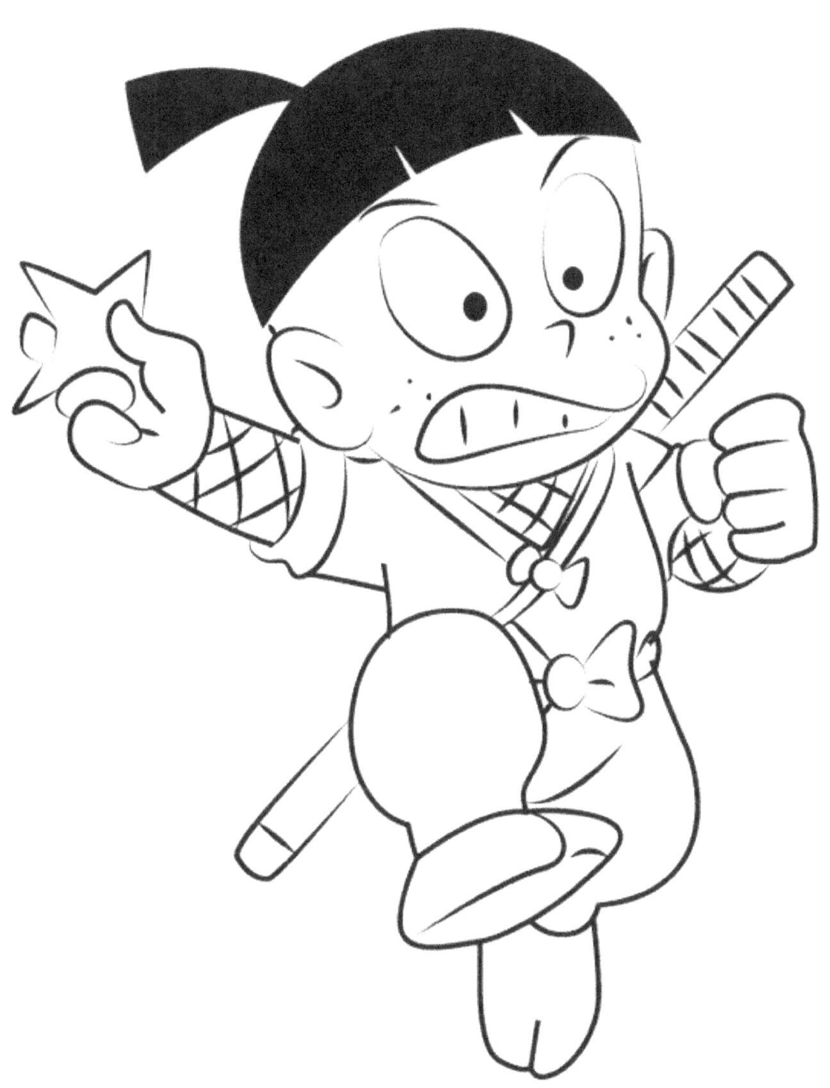

youthbooks

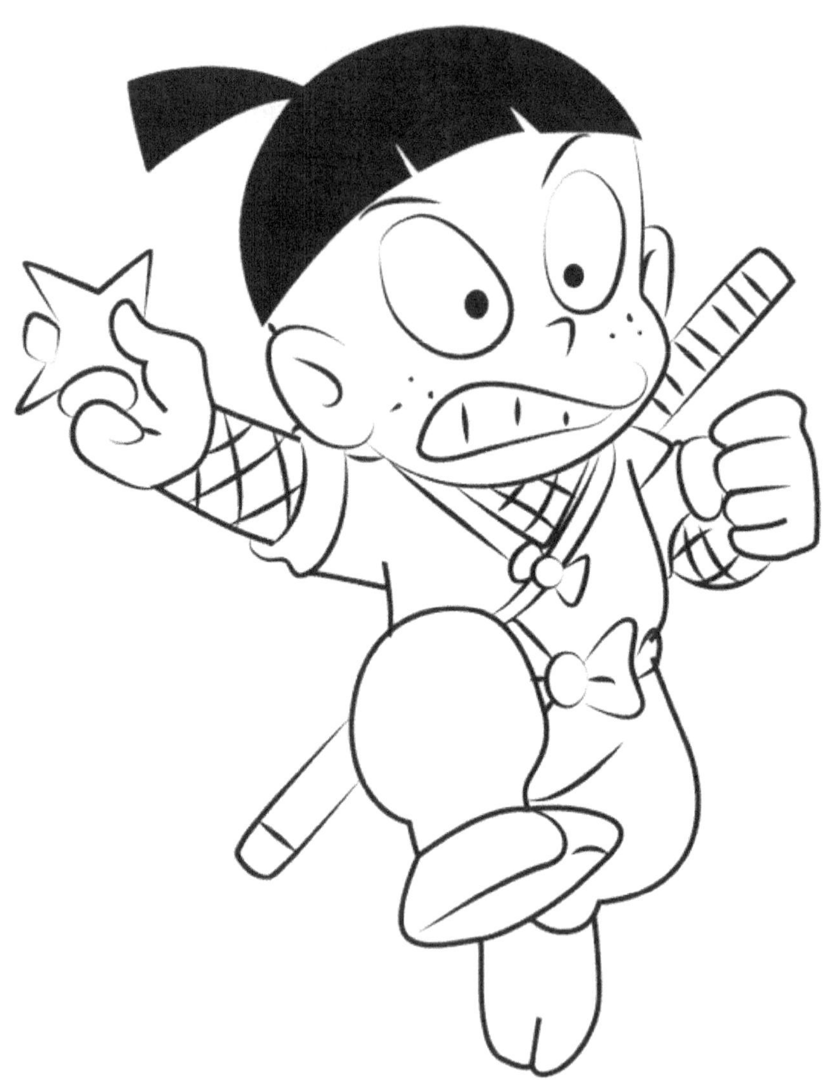

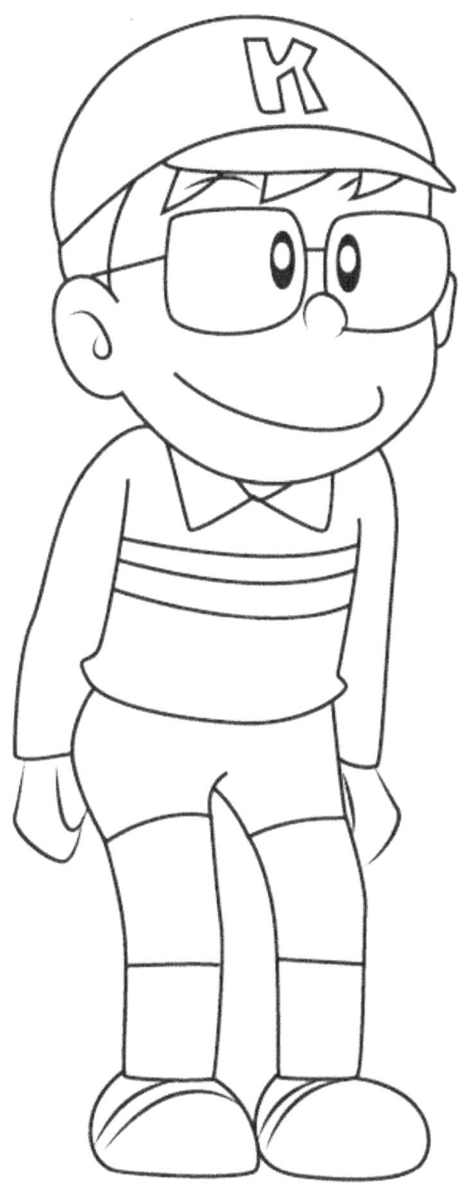

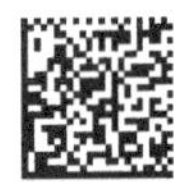

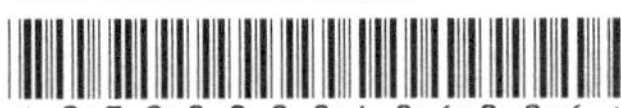
9 798888 496886